A. T. Ariyaratne

Schumacher Lectures
on

BUDDHIST
ECONOMICS

VISHVA LEKHA
Publishers

41, Lumbini Avenue,
Ratmalana
1999

First Edition - 1999

©**Dr. A. T. Ariyaratne**

ISBN 955-599-180-4

Printed and Published in Sri Lanka by

VISHVA LEKHA
41 Lumbini Mawatha Ratmalana

Contents

Charts

INTRODUCTION

In this small book, the lectures given by Dr. A. T. Ariyaratne at the Schumacher College in 1998 January are presented. The theme he has selected is Buddhist Economics and the practical application of Buddhist Economic theory into practice by the Sri Lanka Sarvodaya Movement. To our knowledge, there is no other practical programme in which Buddhist Economic theories are put into practice.

Buddhist teachings have not developed an Economic theory in one place. In different texts, Economic matters are mentioned, and collating all these, a substantial Buddhist Economic theory could be discovered. Dr. Ariyaratne has undertaken the difficult task of collecting such fragments and has woven them into a theory. He does not stop here, but processes further by translating that theory into practice in the Sarvodaya programme.

It was Dr. Schumacher who devoted his attention to Buddhist Economics. Right Livelihood in Buddhism deals with Buddhist Economics. Dr. Ariyaratne has interpreted it to mean the self-effort and the co-operation of all. In Buddhism, self-effort counts first, and no help or assistance from even a God could enable one to reach Nirvana. Self-effort is thus at the basis of Economic development. Together with it is the co-operation of all. No community could develop without all people in that community joining together to develop themselves.

In one Jataka, it is stated how through co-operative efforts a group of birds saved themselves from a hunter. The hunter's net was carried away by them, acting together. Any problem - even economic problems could thus be solved by co-operative effort. The Sarvodaya groups in the village, beginning from the children to adults teach this co-operative effort to everyone.

Buddhist Economics emphasize sharing. Such sharing is extended to material as well as non-material items such as knowledge. The Sarvodaya programme has sharing as its basis, and it had shown how this Buddhist principle could be engaged in order to reap practical results.

The Buddhist Vinaya texts refers to four basic needs, i.e. food, clothing, shelter and medicaments. The Sarvodaya recognizes these basic needs and attempts to satisfy them in every human being. Today, these basic needs are extended to ten in order to include other needs. But today's Sarvodaya attempts to keep away excessive needs thus ensuring a simple life.

To those who desire to read about the Buddhist Economic theory, Dr. Ariyaratne's contribution would be a rewarding experience. It is made much meaningful by giving the reader an insight into the Sarvodaya programme attempting to translate Buddhist economic theory into practice. It is a unique experience; something that one could "See and Feel" in a Sarvodaya village. Could there be a new vision for us in the present world? Is it possible for us to get an inspiration from the Buddhist Economic theory as well as from its practical application in the Sarvodaya programme. If we could do it - then certainly Dr. Ariyaratne's labour had not been in vain.

Professor Nandasena Ratnapala.

Lecture One:
Introduction to Buddhist Economics

I am not an economist. Neither do I claim to be a Buddhist scholar. Then you may wonder why I accepted the invitation from Satish Kumar, Programme Director of Schumacher College, to conduct a course on the theme of Buddhist Economics.

I always believed that to teach is to learn. During the two decades or so I taught late teenagers, mostly at Nalanda College in Colombo, Sri Lanka, I realized that the best way to learn is to teach others as best as I could what I thought I knew. After resigning from my formal teaching profession in 1972 · I continued to be a voluntary community educator to this day mostly among the poorest and powerless people in my country and sometimes in several other countries. A real teacher learns more from those students whom he teaches than the students themselves. So in actual fact I accepted this invitation firstly because I want to learn from you. You are well-educated adults. All of you are my teachers who should assist me by critically anlayzing the experiences and thoughts I will be sharing with you while I am here.

I belong to the Sarvodaya Shramadana Movement of Sri Lanka. Sarvodaya Shramadana means the Awakening of All by the voluntary Sharing of Labour and other resources. The declared Objective of the Movement is:

"To generate a non-violent revolution towards the creation of a Sarvodaya Social Order which will ensure the total awakening of human personalities, human families, village communities, urban communities, national communities and the world community."

Over a period of forty years we have worked very hard to realize this objective by organizing hundreds of activities in thousands of places with the participation of tens of thousands of people. We did not have a ready made theory to follow and neither were we interested in academic theses. On the other hand our cultural values and practices most of which had their roots in the Buddhist teachings had a tremendous influence on our thinking and the way we set about doing things.

Next to the teachings of the Buddha, the Sarvodaya Movement of Sri Lanka was influenced by the non-violent struggles of Mahatma Gandhi and his leading disciples such as Acharya Vinoba Bhave and Sri Jayaprakash Narayan in India.

Today Sarvodaya has evolved a set of principles and guidelines, including some that guide our economic activities. So I felt the opportunity that was given to me by the Schumacher College to talk about Buddhist Economics should not be missed as this may be the most appropriate place and you the most appropriate persons with whom I can share my experiences and thoughts to get your inputs when carving out our future directions. This is the second reason I accepted this invitation.

From early 1972 I knew Dr. E. F. Schumacher personally. He visited our Sarvodaya Headquarters in Sri Lanka and I have been at his home in England on two occasions. I was one of those fortunate persons to have read "Small is Beautiful" in manuscript form and urged him to get it published. Immediately after he got it published we in Sarvodaya with his permission brought out the Sinhala publication. He was a dear friend in whose memory this College was established. That is enough reason for me to accept this invitation.

Once we met in Vienna at an international conference on voluntary services where both of us had to deliver keynote addresses. For several days in the Ausberg Palace where we stayed and strolling in the surrounding parks I drew my best from his wisdom.

In the University of Nijmegan in the Netherlands I was to respond to a speech he was to deliver to an international audience of academics which consisted of several hundreds of participants. It was in February 1976 and was an Appropriate Technology Congress organized by TOOL, a Dutch Appropriate Technology Group. Just five minutes before we were to start there was a telephone call from him from London asking the organizers to get me to speak on the subject as his flight was delayed by a couple of hours so that he could respond to what I said when he finally arrived. I was totally shaken and taken aback but he called me to the phone and reassured me that I could do it. I had no choice and I went to the podium and spoke.

What came to my rescue was what I had learnt when I was less than ten years of age at the Sunday Dhamma School. To my mind came four principles that Lord Buddha advocated when we are engaged in economic activities. I spoke on these. When Fritz came to the meeting and listened to the recording of my speech he mischievously looked at me and said that he was happy to have got delayed. You can read this speech in my Collected Works Volume II, Chapter. 5.

I was trying to build up a self- development movement of the people, by the people and for the people and it was Dr. Schumacher who by his famous Chapter on Buddhist Economics who inspired me to look deeply at Buddha's teachings to discover the economic principles on which Sarvodaya movement should be guided. I should not forget also my dear friend George McRobie who taught me so much on the subject that Small is Possible. After the untimely and sudden demise of Dr. Schumacher I was asked by the Schumacher Society to deliver the Schumacher Lecture in Bristol in November 1984. This talk on A No Poverty Society, which I delivered, is published in my Collected Works Volume III Chapter 11. During the course of my stay here I will try to share with you what I learnt on this subject by applying Buddhist principles into actual practice over a period of 40 years in social, economic and political life of the people of our country.

Unlike me Prof. Sulak Sivaraksa who will continue this course on Buddhist Economics after I leave is both a scholar and an activist. As the creator of the concept of Engaged Buddhism he has probed much into this subject. His profound knowledge on Buddhism and international political and economic processes should be fully tapped by you when he is here. I am happy he is associated with this course as a better-qualified person to perform this task.

The entire treatment of the subject of Buddhist Economics by me will be from an experiential point of view of Sarvodaya. Academic treatment of a subject was never of interest to me. I always tried to discover ways and means of putting any knowledge into serving the people. Knowledge that does not help people to overcome their problems and lead a better and happier life is of no use.

The economic life of a human being cannot be separated from his total life and living. Buddha Dhamma looks at a life as a whole. In fact the entire living world is treated as a whole in Buddha's teachings.

Without this holistic understanding of life it is difficult for humans to follow the path to happiness, He showed. Economics is only a fragment of life and living. Therefore moral and social implications of economic activity cannot be considered apart from economics. The Buddhist approach to problems is holistic, empirical and practical. The Buddha's message was to the whole of humanity and therefore

- 3 -

transcends all barriers of religion, race, colour, national boundaries and political ideologies. It is a teaching directed to the awakening and well-being of all.

Sarvodaya means the Awakening of All - from an individual Human Personality to Humanity as a whole. This awakening has spiritual, moral, cultural, social, economic and political dimensions. Whatever we do in one of these sectors influences all other sectors.

When we work towards the welfare of all the means we use have to be based on Truth, Non-violence and Selflessness in conformity with Awakening of All. Even when economic activities are carried out they have to conform to these basic tenets. In other words Buddhist economics cannot dispense with its ethical foundations. Economics in Buddhism is not a plethora of slogans and catch words like raising the national income, increasing productive and purchasing power, improving efficiency and creating full employment. Values like discipline, awareness and wisdom cannot be dispensed with in any human activity that follows Buddha's teachings.

Having analyzed the Noble Truth of Suffering, The Noble Truth of the Causes that bring about Suffering and the Noble Truth of Cessation of Suffering, Lord Buddha explains the Noble Truth of the Path that leads to the Cessation of Suffering. This is the Noble Eight-fold Path.

The Noble Eight-fold Path which is also known as the Middle Path has eight steps or components which includes everything pertaining to the spheres of our thoughts, words and deeds. We have to look at these in totality one in relationship to the others. The Noble Eight-fold Path is:

- Right Understanding
- Right Words
- Right Livelihood
- Right Awareness and
- Right Thoughts
- Right Deeds
- Right Effort
- Right Concentration.

Schumacher begins his Chapter on Buddhist Economics in Small is Beautiful with the following words:

'Right Livelihood is one of the requirements of the Buddha's Noble Eight-fold Path. It is clear, therefore, that there must be such a thing as Buddhist Economics.'

Later in the same chapter he continues:

'While the materialist is mainly interested in goods, the Buddhist is mainly interested in liberation. But Buddhism is the 'Middle Way' and therefore in no way antagonistic to physical well-being. It is not wealth that stands in the way to liberation but attachment to wealth, not the enjoyment of pleasurable things but the craving for them. The keynote of Buddhist economics, therefore, is simplicity and non-violence.From an economist's point of view, the marvel of the Buddhist way of life is the utter rationality of its pattern - amazingly small means leading to extraordinarily satisfying results.'

Buddha's teachings pertaining to economics, as we understand it today as a specialized subject, was not spelt out by him as a separate treatise, so that when the Dhamma was written down later, one could go straight into it. He did not teach economics. He taught what He discovered by His own efforts while living through several world cycles in many living forms. He taught how we too can overcome the cycles of births and deaths and attain supreme happiness and enlightenment. In other words His teaching was how we could lead this present life in a righteous way so that our Path to deliverance will not be hindered.

Our Buddhist culture taught us from our young days how we should keep in mind our welfare not only in this life but also in the afterlife as well in whatever we think, say or do. Belief in Rebirth and the Karmic Law - Law of Cause and Effect, were two fundamental teachings we were taught to keep in mind. Economics and Politics or any other department of life cannot function without adverse consequences if we resort to unrighteous or wrongful ways. Good ends can be realized only by good means.

The first two stanzas of the Dhammapada explain this philosophy very vividly.

'Mind is the forerunner of (all evil) states. Mind is supreme, mind-made are they. If one speaks or acts with a wicked mind, because of that, suffering follows one, like the wheel follows the hoof of the draught-ox.'

'Mind is the forerunner of (all good) states. Mind is supreme, and mind-made are they. If one speaks or acts with a pure mind, because of that, happiness follows one, like one's shadow that never leaves.'

In spite of the fact that what Buddha primarily taught was a very pragmatic path to spiritual liberation, and his stress on living with awareness every moment 'abstaining from doing evil, cultivating goodness and purifying the mind,' throughout His teachings, the right kind of conduct for personal and human well-being in the social, economic and political spheres is stressed. Therefore what we can do is to get these teachings from various suttas and other references and attempt to synthesize them as a composite whole so that we can apply them as principles of Buddhist economics in our development efforts today.

The Sarvodaya Shramadana Movement of Sri Lanka is referred to by some scholars as Buddhism in Development Action or Engaged Buddhism. It is not purely economic activities we are engaged in. It is a total, holistic and an integrated approach to bring about a non-violent but revolutionary social change. Economic development is included in this. Perhaps it is not far from the truth to say that Sarvodaya is attempting to build 'A No-Poverty No-Affluence Society.' Buddhist approach to solving problems is empirical, practical and holistic. Both material and spiritual development should go hand in hand. All activities economic or otherwise, in Buddhism, are subservient to ethical and moral evaluation.

Schumacher himself points out the difference in approach by modern economists:

"Economists themselves, like most specialists, normally suffer from a kind of metaphysical blindness, assuming that theirs is a science of absolute and invariable truths, without any presuppositions. Some go as far as to claim that economic laws are as free from 'metaphysics' or 'values' as the law of gravitation".

Schumacher ends his chapter on Buddhist Economics with the following words:

"It is in the light of both immediate experience and long-term prospects that the study of Buddhist Economics could be recommended even to those who believe that economic growth is more important than any spiritual or religious values. For it is not a question of choosing between 'modern growth' and 'traditional stagnation.' It is a question of finding the right path of development, the Middle Way between materialist heedlessness and traditionalist immobility, in short, of finding 'Right Livelihood.'

During this course I will try to discuss with you the following themes so that together we can contribute to the current issues on Development Theory and Practice from a Buddhist point of view. I will deal with the subject in relation to the experiments carried out mainly by the Sarvodaya Shramadana Movement of Sri Lanka.

1. Buddhist Teachings on Economic, Political and Social Affairs as these bear on Sarvodaya's Vision.
2. Sarvodaya Ideal of Awakening.
3. Shramadana as a vehicle for actualizing the Sarvodaya Ideal of Awakening.
4. Building a No-poverty Society.
5. Replacing Full-employment with Full-engagement - Right Livelihood
6. Sarvodaya Economic Enterprises Development Services -
7. Globalization with a Humane Approach.
8. Peace through a Sarvodaya Social Order.
9. Awakening in the New Millennium.

Lecture Two:
Buddhist Teachings on Economic, Political and Social Affairs as these bear on Sarvodaya's Vision

At the time of the Buddha, over 2600 years ago, there was no 'Science' of Economics as we find today. Yet most activities that are studied today under the subject of Economics were going on during his time also, though it was a comparatively simple economy. There was production, distribution, consumption, exchange of goods and services, use of money as a medium of exchange, division of labour, profit-making, taxation and so on. That was a period of economic transition where trade was coming in increasingly into a previously agricultural and cattle-breeding economy. In fact there was a new very wealthy class of businessmen who were referred to as settis.

State dominated over the ownership of land while trade and industry were in the hands of the private business class. State got its wealth through taxation while the private sector made money through profit making. People were generally engaged in agriculture, cottage industries and other work that satisfied the basic needs of the community in which they lived. There were others who were employed in state services and in the industrial and business enterprises of the private sector.

Undoubtedly the majority of people would have lived a life outside this organized economy which later-day economists called a subsistence economy. A person like myself would venture to call it more or less a self-sufficient and sustainable economy. Certainly there would have been exploitation and poverty in the midst of a generally No-Poverty society.

Lord Buddha was a realist and a very practical Teacher. His Mission was not to formulate a model political or economic system. He took for granted the systems that existed during His time and analyzed and showed the flaws in those from a spiritual, moral and ethical point of view. Further He advised them on the correct way of doing things for the development of the personality of the individual human being and the society in general. Whenever he was asked or came across situations where His observations on economic and political matters helped people to improve them materially as well as spiritually. He never hesitated to guide them on the correct path. Kings and nobles, settis and commoners benefited from his teachings.

Buddhism accepts freedom from want. For this economic activities are necessary. Even for monks (Bhikkus) and nuns (Bhikkunis) who have renounced house-hold life in search of spiritual pursuits, robes or clothing (civara), food (pindapatha), shelter (senasana) and medicinal wherewithal (gilanapratya) are necessary. Both monks and nuns, and laymen and women, need a conducive environment to live (patirupa desa vasoca). Even in the most primitive societies human beings cannot survive without these basic needs. Buddha appreciated and understood these needs and clearly taught them how to earn their livelihood justly (anavajjāni kammāni), and how to utilize their earnings for the benefit of oneself and others.

As societies developed and production of commodities and services increased, then to this portfolio of basic human needs several others were added such as energy requirements, communication, education and cultural needs. As human civilizations advanced more and more in the fields of science and technology certain secondary and tertiary needs were required to be satisfied. Need-based economies were slowly transformed into want-based economies and then, as the modern times approached, especially after the industrial revolution and colonialism, we witnessed how a greed-based economy came into being and made geometrical progressions. This has brought about a devastating impact on human society and environment and as we reach the Third Millennium (of the Christian Era) we witness that we are now ready to make a quantum jump into total oblivion. We are examining 'Buddhist Economics' at a critical time like this.

Lord Buddha did not preach class antagonism. On the other hand He clearly taught that the greatness of an individual did not depend on his wealth but on his character. The question is not whether an individual is rich or poor but whether he is good or bad, virtuous or sinful. It is one's actions - kamma - that qualitatively determine the greatness of a person. If one earns wealth by sinful and wrong means such a person does lot of harm to himself and others. True happiness will evade him. Similarly one should spend what one has earned wisely.

Buddha was not against earning wealth the right way, by Right Actions (Sammā Kammantha). In fact this is one of the eight steps in the Noble Eight-fold Path. He gave advice on how best to earn wealth. He mentioned vigorous effort and great enthusiasm as essential qualities to be developed by those who want to acquire wealth. The idle can never be rich. Wealth has to be earned by lawful and just means. The Buddha, compares one who does not strive and remain poor through idleness and lack of enthusiasm to a person blind in both eyes; one who becomes rich by wrong means (Miccā Kammantha) is like a person having one eye (eka cakku); one who has become rich by good means is compared to a man with both eyes (dvi cakku).

In the Samyutta Nikāya it is observed that wealth can be earned by three means (1) Unlawfully and by violence, (2) Unlawfully and lawfully by violence and non-violence, (3) Lawfully and without violence. The third way is advocated as the best to be followed by the wise and those pursue true happiness. Similarly, a successful businessman will have to develop (1) Skill in buying and selling, (2) A sense of net profit, (3) Ready sources of capital, (4) A service geared to the satisfaction of consumers, and (5) Diligent work discipline.

In the Vyaggapajja Sutta Buddha advises householders to keep in mind and practice four principles that lead to happiness on earth. Advising Dighajānu who raised the question of householders' happiness on earth Buddha says: (1) Cultivate skills, be efficient, earnest and devoted to your profession (Uttānasampadā), (2) Carefully protect what you have earned with your efforts righteously (Ārakkhasampadā), (3) Associate only with wise, virtuous and good friends (Kalyānamittatā), and Live a life of economic evenness and choose the right style of living (Samajivikatā).

In Buddhist texts and related literature numerous instances can be found pertaining to making wealth in the right way. Then, what are the wrong ways of earning money? They are by taking away life, by thieving, by deception, by producing and selling intoxicating substances and drugs, poisons and weapons that destroy human and animal life and property and trading in slaves. In Buddhist economics this kind of economic activity is totally unacceptable. Imagine what will happen to our national and world economic statistics that measure standards of living of people by growth rates, per capita incomes and GDP's etc. if only our governments follow Buddhist Economic Principles!

Buddha's greatest lay disciple was a setthi named Anāthapindika. It was he who bought the land and constructed the famous Jetawanā monastery at

Sāvatthi. Anāthapindika was a great banker too. Once describing what is happiness for a layman Buddha mentioned four kinds of happiness to him. Firstly, when by righteous means wealth is acquired and owned by a person there is a great sense of economic security and self-esteem (atthisukha); secondly, the feeling that he could spend that wealth as he wishes on himself, his family, his friends and relatives, his workers and on meritorious deeds (bhoga-sukha); thirdly, to be free from debts (anana-sukha) and fourthly to live a life of purity in thought word and deed (anavajja-sukkha). See how Buddha balances the first three, which are economic with the last, which is spiritual.

Buddha spelt out five spheres in which wealth should be spent, namely, for self-happiness, happiness of others, self-defence, state dues and taxes, and meritorious deeds.

A very popular advice by the Buddha about the ways one should get about with earnings is found in the Sigālovada Sutta:

Spend one portion of the earnings for consumption purposes (Ekene Bhoge Bhunjeyya).

Invest two portions in business or industry (Dvihi kamman payojayē),

Save one portion to be used if and when in distress (Chatuttampi Nidāpeyya, Āpadasu Bhavissati).

Buddha in his preachings gave the pride of place to women in managing the household economy. 'She knows the household work best and is capable. She can manage the servants well. She has pleasing ways towards the husband and she guards his wealth'.

In the Parābhava Sutta four ways of losing wealth are mentioned (apāyamukhani). These are Looseness with women (ittidutta), debauchery (surādutta), gambling (akkhadutta), and evil friends (pāpamitta).

Again in the Sigālovada sutta six ways of losing wealth and succumbing to suffering is explained. These are 1. Addiction to intoxicants, 2. Frequenting the streets at unseemly hours, 3. Haunting fairs, 4. Getting infatuated by gambling, 5. Associating with evil companions and 6. Idle company. Six perils that entail each of these are described in detail.

The first results in loss of wealth, increase in quarrels, susceptibility to disease, loss of reputation and good character, indecent exposure and impaired intelligence.

The second causes insecurity to him, his wife, children and property, can become suspicious of crimes, cause false rumours around him, and endless other troubles.

The third is a restless mind thinking all the time where dancing, singing, music, recitation, merrymaking etc are going on.

Fourth attracts hatred by winning, sadness by losing, wasted life, not trusted in a court of law, despised by officials and friends, not considered to give or take in marriage.

The fifth is taking as friends any gambler, libertine, tippler, swindler, cheat, or criminal.

Sixth, the idler finds excuses not to work saying it is too early; too late, too cold, too hot, too hungry, too full etc and work remains undone, wealth is drained away while getting no income.

From these examples we see scattered through out the teachings of the Buddha valuable principles relating to production, distribution and consumption of wealth and how it should be done and the right and wrong ways of using it. Underlying all these is the objective of the well-being of the individual person, the family, the community, the entire society and nature. Equal empahsis is given to material as well as spiritual well-being. Therefore the moral laws such as the Kammic Laws of Causality should govern all our activities including the economic.

In Buddhism human labour is recognized as a fundamental source of wealth. But labour is much more than added monetary value to a natural resource. It transcends the employer - employee relations as far as remuneration is concerned. What is important is every human being being engaged in righteous work. Physical work is as important as mental work in the awakening of human personality. Every person has the right to choose the work according to his feelings and abilities and develop his faculties. When working with other people in bringing about goods and services needed for the well-being of the community a person overcomes his egocentredness. Buddhism accepts division of labour and specialization but totally rejects the concept of judging a human being as high and low from the work he does. By birth one does not become a high caste or low caste, but by actions alone one becomes a brahmin or an outcaste. Buddha discarded the caste-oriented employment system.

Organizing and training labour; looking into their age, sex, and physical fitness; their contentment, high morality, welfare, leave, medical care, reasonable wages and incentives; and motivation of labour are all mentioned in Buddhist teachings.

Buddha's concern was for all beings, their relationships to one another and nature extending to the entire universal phenomena. Therefore, he laid down five Cosmic (Universal) Laws (Niyāma Dhammas) that grovern all other man-made laws and therefore should fall within them if human beings are to survive in this world and live in peace and happiness. They are the ones pertaining to the Genes (Bīja), Seasons (Utu), Causal chain (Kamma), Phenomena (Dhamma) and Mind (Citta).

There are three suttas, namely, the Cakkavattasihanada sutta, Kutadanta sutta and the Aggañña sutta detailing out economic and political processes that bring about peace and prosperity or conflict and disaster. They are very relevant even today. The entire economic structure can crumble and plunge a country into chaos and destruction if production decreases and there is maldistribution of goods and wealth. This is where State intervention is necessary and remedial action should be taken. A handful of persons are not allowed to hoard the wealth of a country. What is necessary is a holistic approach and not haphazard patch-work. Wealth should not be wasted on festivities and rural wealth should not be drained out to the cities for these festivities. Kutadanta sutta advocates a decentralised monetary system. Natural resources and national wealth should be preserved and methodical planning and constructive ventures should be implemented. In the same way that when economic changes took place in the form of private property and organized farming, cattle-breeding and industry there were appropriate administrative and social developments like the election of a King, similarly, required and appropriate political measures should be taken to cope with changes that occur in the economic field.

One may acquire and use wealth in the right ways still the danger of losing all this from fire, water, kings, robbers, enemies and heirs is always there. Nothing is everlasting. Everything is subject to change. Therefore, Buddha cautions us: Decline follows the man who is proud of his wealth. Wisdom is better than Wealth (Tamahi panna dhanena seyya - Majjima Nikāya). Supreme wealth is Happiness (Santhutti paramam dhanam - Dhammapada).

There is a wealth that is not subject to the above dangers and cannot be taken away by anybody else. These are: Wealth of Faith (Saddhādāna), Wealth of Virtue (Sīladāna), Wealth of Conscientiousness (Hiridana), Wealth of Fear of Blame (Ottappadāna), Wealth of listening (Sutadāna), Wealth of Beneficence (Cagadāna) and Wealth of Wisdom (Paññadāna).

So far I have dealt with some Buddhist textual material related to the subject of Economics. I have not tried so far to find out how far these are applicable to modern times. Neither have I attempted to compare these teachings with what generally goes as Economic 'Science' today. I put the word science in quote because I am not convinced of the way that as it is studied and applied today that it is a science the way I look at science. In the lectures that follow I will describe how the Sarvodaya Shramadana Movement in Sri Lanka has been trying to face the challenging issues of the day following the above guidelines enunciated by the Buddha over 2500 years ago.

❧⚜❧

Ten Duties of King

First - *Dāna*

The first of the "Ten Duties of the King' is liberality, generosity (*Dāna*). The ruler should not have craving and attachment to wealth and property, but should give it away for the welfare of the people.

Second - *Sīla*

A high moral character (*Sīla*). He should never destroy life, cheat, steal and exploit others, commit adultery, utter falsehood, and take intoxicating drinks. That is, he must at least observe the five Precepts of the layman.

Third - *Pariccāga*

Sacrificing everything for the good of the people. (*Pariccāgā*), he must be prepared to give up all personal comfort, name and fame, and even his life, in the interest of the people.

Fourth - *Ajjava*

Honesty and integrity (*Ajjava*). He must be free of fear or favour in the discharge of his duties, must be sincere in his intentions, and must not deceive the public.

Fifth - *Maddava*

Kindness and gentleness (*Maddava*). He must possess a genial temperament.

Six - *Tapa*

Austerity in habits (*Tapa*). He must lead a simple life, and should not indulge in a life of luxiry. He must have self-control.

Seven - *Akkodha*

Freedom from hatred, ill-will, enmity (*Akkodha*). He should not bear any grudge against anybody.

Eight - *Avihimsā*

Non-violence (*Avihimsā*), which means not only that he should not harm anybody, but also that he should try to promote peace by avoiding and preventing war, and everything which involves violence and destruction of life.

Nine - *Kanthi*

Patience, forbearance, tolerance, understanding (*Kanthi*). He must be able to bear hardship, difficulties and insults without losing his temper.

Ten - *Avirodha*

Non-opposition, non-obstruction (*Avirodha*), that is to say that he should not oppose the will of the people, should not obstruct any measures that are conducive to the welfare of the people. In other words he should rule in harmony with his people.

Lecture Three:
The Sarvodaya Ideal of Awakening

In Buddhist literature a word very frequently used is 'Sabba.' Sabba means all, everything. This is in Pali language. The Sanskrit word is 'Sarva.' Similarly 'Metta' in Pali or 'Maitree' in Sanskrit means respect or friendliness. I would say the foundation of a good, contented, and peaceful society, where the human being, the society and nature can survive harmoniously is expressed in these two words, "Sabba and Metta,' - Respect for All life or Friendliness towards All. The word Sarvodaya, coined by Mahatma Gandhi, meaning Welfare of All, was adopted by us in Sri Lanka, to express this meaning which we slightly amended as the Awakening of All to keep in line with the Buddhist spirit of Awakening. The Buddha means the Awakened One.

Any human being or society, and in fact the entire humanity, should have the highest possible common ideal before its mind based on a flawless vision if we are to overcome the present day miseries, uncertainties and sufferings. Sarvodaya is the ideal and the vision chosen by us. In the Karanīyametta Sutta (the Discourse on Loving Kindness) the Buddha uses the expression 'Dittin ca Anupagamma Silavā Dassanena Sampanno kāmesu vineyya gedham' which means 'without falling into erroneous views, virtuous, endowed with vision, and conquering sensual pleasures.' A clarity of vision is needed to understand problems, perceive causes that gave rise to them, develop strategies to remove the causes, release corrective processes and to take stock of successes and failures so that adjustments can be made.

The latest slogan some use nowadays is globalization promising it as the panacea for all the world's ills. It is true that the horizons of the world are contracting physically as a result of advancement of transport and communication systems and expansion of free movement of goods and services in a worldwide market. However this same developments will widen the material gap between the poor and the powerless and the rich and the powerful unless the spiritual emptiness that generally exists in the latter is filled with beneficence, love and selflessness. Bringing home this truth is next to impossible with the rich and powerful for a Movement like Sarvodaya however much we try. Yet the poor and the powerless are numerically more and are within the reach of Sarvodaya. So our endeavours must necessarily and primarily be with the poor and the powerless people to gather the needed momentum for a global application, which includes all.

Our task is the more difficult because unlike the free-market economy or political alignments like the European Community, ASEAN or SAARC, our mandate is not from man-made political and economic arrangements, but is derived from our innermost spiritual aspirations and moral values and a vision we share to bring about happiness for all transcending caste, class, color, creed, race, religious, political, national and other barriers. One may call this very idealistic and that is right, though partly, yet we are also very practical as one can see from the track record of what we have achieved.

Long before the present form of globalization, with its promises of material prosperity and its sustainability, was given expression to and was accepted by the elite, and projected to the poor as the newest and surest way to solve their problems, the common people of the villages in our country for over two millennia had accepted the thought or vision of eradicating the physical and mental suffering and fear from all sentient beings. They were promoters of a global consciousness of oneness of mankind. The exact words of two Pali stanzas they recite in their daily religious observances to this day are as follows:

1. May there be seasonal rains   "Devo vassatu kālena
    May there be agricultural prosperity   Sassa sampatthi hotuca
    May the entire living world be happy   Pito bhavatu lokoca
    May the rulers be righteous   Rajā bhavatu dhammikā" (Pāli)

2. May those who suffer physically overcome their suffering.
    May those who are in fear overcome their fear
    May those who suffer mentally overcome their pain
    May all living beings be well and happy.

    "Dukkhappattāca niddhukkā; Bhayappattāca nibbaya;
    Sokappattaca nissoka; Honthu sabbepi pānino. (Pali)

What do these daily religious invocations mean in practical terms? Human beings should have the well-being of all as their foremost wish. In other words they should have Loving Kindness and Compassion in their minds and hearts. Not only oneness of humanity but the inter-relatedness of all sentient beings and the importance of natural cycles must be accepted and appreciated. Agriculture should be promoted understanding how seasons work and making proper use of water. Those who suffer due to lack of physical needs like water, food, clothing, shelter, medicines and so on should be helped. Those who are bereaved due to ignorance of reality or the Dhamma should be educated and consoled. Those who are subjected to fear due to various causes like injustices, natural disasters, wars and denial of human rights etc should be assisted. All these things should be done with an understanding of the interdependence and interrelatedness between us all and nature and directed towards realizing happiness to oneself and others.

The kind of value system I mentioned now probably governed the life of communities of an earlier era. With the passage of time, principles which were practiced became mere slogans. The "value system' probably existed in the collective memory of the people. Sarvodaya has revived it and made it very practical in the modern context.

How can we put these concepts into a form that could be easily practiced? How can we organise them in such a way that they get motivated by their own cultural values and learn to take their own decisions in matters affecting their own lives? How can we help them to build their own community-based and community-managed structures that ensure security pertaining to their Basic Human Needs? How can we network these basic organizations, structures and processes released by them progressively and non-violently in such a way that they can influence the national and global trends for a more equitable, sustainable and peaceful existence for themselves as well as others?

These are the underlying questions for which we in Sarvodaya have had to find satisfactory and working solutions as the Movement expanded during the last four decades from one village community to over 10,000 villages.

If we look at the above mentioned inspirational stanzas chanted daily by the common people what do they highlight? The first one highlights; seasonal rains that naturally fall, agricultural prosperity that has to be achieved by man's efforts, accepting the right of all sentient and living beings to live (loko here includes even the plant kingdom), and justice from the hands of the rulers. The second stanza highlights the purpose for which the above resources have to be used, namely, for the weal and happiness of all living beings. What are the factors that prevent the well-being and happiness of living beings? They are physical and mental sufferings and fear.

As long as forests are not indiscriminately cut down, rivers, streams and other water resources are protected and in short nature is respected and conserved there will be seasonal rains. In these lines which is a part of our cultural heritage we find the philosophical basis on which water reservoirs and irrigation systems were constructed and the country was made self-sufficient in food. In fact they exported the surplus to other countries. Astronomical and astrological sciences were also utilized not in a superstitious way but in a very pragmatic way in relation to all the stages of farming, from clearing and ploughing the land to harvesting storing and consumption.

For example the three principles adopted in agriculture were, working according to auspicious times (neketha), working collectively to help one another (kayya) and sharing (panguwa). The present day objectives of efficiency, management and equity were built into the cultural lives of the people without much external intervention. The king or the rulers came into the picture when they gave leadership and assistance of the state to construct the giant irrigation tanks and irrigation canals with the participation of the people. There was no slave labour. It was a willing sacrifice on the part of the rulers and the people for their welfare in this life and lives to come. The material objective was survival and happiness in this life and the spiritual objective was the conviction that the surplus merit gathered in doing community service in this life will help them in the future lives.

Compassion towards all life was at the heart of this kind of community life. There was no question of choosing between violence and non-violence. Non-violence was the accepted norm. This did not mean that to defend their freedom and way of life against violent invaders they would remain passive and submit. Rather they took up arms and defended themselves against any invasion from outside. They wished their king to be righteous. What is meant by righteousness is the adherence of the king to the Ten Principles of Good Governance (Dasa Rāja

Dharma).

These are:

Dāna	Beneficence or Sharing
Sīla	Morality
Pariccāga	Donations
Ajjawam	Uprightness
Majjawam	Impartiality
Tapam	Composure
Akkodo	Non-hatred
Avihimsā	Non-violence
Khanthi	Forgiveness
Avirodhatā	Non-revengefulness

What is physical suffering (dukkha)? Not having enough water to drink and food to eat, insufficient health and medical care, lack of a proper shelter to live and not having minimum clothes to wear are all different forms of physical suffering. We can say people physically suffer when they do not have their physical needs satisfied. What is fear? When people have to live in an environment where Basic Human Rights are denied and they are subjected to physical harassment, torture and even death they are in constant fear (bhaya). What is mental suffering? People may not suffer physically or may not live in an environment stricken with fear. Yet they may mentally suffer due to ignorance of the Dhamma - the truth of reality. It is this context that the teachings of the Buddha becomes indispensable for a society and its people who are in pursuit of a happiness transcending so-called physical and mental health. The ultimate shared goal of such a society is 'Hontu Sabbepi Pāṅino - May all beings be well and happy.'

What we try to achieve in contemporary society by way of fundamental rights, basic needs, democracy, rule of law, justice and equity, environmental conservation and ecological balance, peace and tolerance and so on are all condensed in the two stanzas cited above. Four Hundred and Fifty years of foreign subjugation and fifty years of foreign imitation by our rulers and planners have resulted in our losing this value base and cultural heritage. Today in every respect we are suffering. However the Sarvodaya Shramadana Movement in Sri Lanka has tried to bring the left over pieces together and build up a working model from these roots for the last four decades.

The central concept of Development as conceived, accepted and implemented by Sarvodaya is based on this Buddhist spirit. Yet it has within its followers people of all religious faiths. Sarvodaya is not opposed to any religion. On the contrary in the same Buddhist spirit Sarvodaya respects all religions. According to Sarvodaya, Development is an awakening process. This awakening process should begin with human personalities and extend to families, peer groups, village and urban communities, national communities and the world community. As the idea spreads and the movement expands each of these awakening processes enhances the others, slowly building up a critical mass which is needed for a real social transformation. So we put down the Objective of the Sarvodaya Movement as follows:

To generate a non-violent total revolution towards the creation of a Sarvodaya Social Order, which will ensure the total awakening of: - Human Personalities (Pūrna Paurushodaya), Human Families (Kutumbodaya), Village Communities (Grāmodaya), Urban Communities (Nagarōdaya), National Communities (Deshōdaya) and the World Community (Vishvōdaya).

Here priority is given to the quality of human personality and not to the material things at his disposal. A country may have the highest growth rate and people may enjoy a very high material standard of living yet they may have high suicidal or homicidal rates at the same time. They may not have the degree of happiness that a less prosperous community of people enjoys. Sarvodaya considers that every human being should strive to awaken his or her personality to the fullest to get optimum happiness in this life.

According to Buddhism our life is a combination of Mind (nāma) and Matter (rūpa). It is the co-existence of mind and matter that we call sentient life. Mind consists of the sum total of sensations, perceptions, volitions and consciousness while matter consists of a combination of the four elements, namely, solidity, fluidity, motion and heat. It is the combination of these two elements of mind and matter the functioning of which give rise to what we call human personality. When mind and matter ceases to co-exist and are separated it is called death. Rebirth is a recombination of mental elements in a different recombination of material elements. An understanding of this process of becoming and dissolving, arising and passing away, subject to the Law of Dependent Co-arising is the key to self-realization. It is the One Way (Ekāyana Magga) to unravel the mystery of birth, disease, old age, death and re-birth cycle. A human being who diligently tries to understand and break this cycle of births and deaths (Sansāric Cycle) to achieve unconditioned happiness is the ideal human being who is truly on the path to personality awakening.

Self-realization is a long and arduous process which needs lot of mental, verbal and bodily discipline and, patience and effort. Only a very few people in a community will have the urge and energy to tread a path of this nature. Yet they can motivate most if not all the other people in their community to respect the importance of this under-standing and cultivate as much of it while living the normal house-holders life.

In fact even in our childhood we remember our parents, grand-par-ents and other elders practicing the Ānāpanasati Bhāvanā (meditation on the process of breathing in and breathing out) to develop one-point-edness of mind or concentration, Metta Bhāvanā (meditation on lov-ing-kindness), Anicca Bhāvanā (meditation on impermance) and final-ly Vipassanā Bhāvanā (Insight meditation). These were the 'spiritual technologies' they used to conquer their inner cravings, aversions and ignorance.

For a Buddhist the ultimate and supreme happiness is the attain-ment of Nibbānam Paramam Sukham. Nibbāna is the highest point in the awakening of human personality. Nibbana is the cessation of becoming. Thereafter there will be no rebirth after death. The cycle of births and deaths that gives rise to all forms of suffering comes to an end to a person who attains nibbana or enlightenment.

Attainment of Nibbāna is a very distant goal for most of the Buddhists. It may take a numerous number of births and deaths. Yet the beginning has to be made here and now in this life. While the Buddha showed us the way to supreme happiness He was concerned very much with our present. If we miss the present we will certainly miss the future. So when the Buddha said 'Nibbanam paramam sukham' He preceded that sentence with three other sentences of wisdom pertain-ing to this life.

Arogyā parama lābhā	Good health is the greatest blessing
Santhuti paramam dhanam	Contentment is the greatest wealth
Viswāsa paramā gññāti	Trust is the greatest relation
Nibbanam paramam sukham	Nibbāna is the greatest happiness.

The challenge that Sarvodaya accepted is to develop the philosophy, the principles and programmes based on this wisdom, and modern scientific knowledge and appropriate technology. The outcome is an early childhood development programmes, children's programmes, mothers' programmes, youth programmes and elders' programmes and so on to promote physical, emotional, mental, spiritual, social and environment health; improvement of livelihood schemes with checks and balances to prevent greed overpowering contentment; and economic development programmes where competition and accumulative instincts are replaced with mutuality and trust.

In Sarvodaya we have the human being at the centre of all development. His or her personality awakening is the ultimate objective. Different human beings may be at different stages of this awakening. A facilitating or enabling environment at the family, group, community, national or world levels is necessary for the human personality to awaken. In other words all other forms and levels of development also are defined as awakening processes in Sarvodaya terminology. A Global Framework - Planning for Awakening can be presented as follows:

A GLOBAL FRAMEWORK - PLANNING FOR AWAKENING

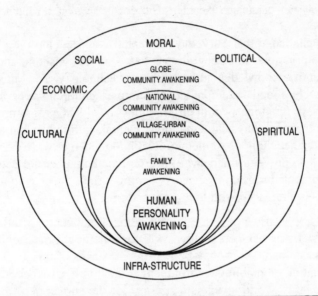

BIOSPHERE	- PORTION OF THE EARTH WHERE LIFE OCCURS
ECO-SYSTSEM	- INTER-DEPENDENT BIOTIC AND NON-BIOTIC COMPONENTS
PSYCHOSPHERE	- SUM TOTAL OF PSYCHIC ENERGIES RADIATED BY HUMAN CONSCIOUSNESS
	COSMIC LAWS GOVERNING HUMAN LIFE

Lecture Four:
Shramadana as a vehicle for actualizing the Sarvodaya Ideal of Awakening

The four Sublime Abodes (Satara Brahma Viharana) and the four Modes of Social Conduct (Satara Sanghraha Vastu) that the Buddha taught can be easily understood and followed by the common people if psychological, physical and social conditions can be created to practice these. The practice of these principles helps in the personality awakening processes of individuals, groups, families and communities. The Sarvodaya Movement in communities creates such a psycho-physical and social environment by organizing Shramadāna Camps, Shramadāna literally means donation or sharing (dāna) of labour (shrama). We have given a broader meaning to shramadāna as 'an act of sharing one's time, thought, effort and other resources with the community' for the awakening of oneself and others. This is the reason why the movement is popularly known as the Sarvodaya Shramadāna Movement of Sri Lanka.

Sarvodaya has recognised Ten Basic Human Needs that have to be satisfied for human beings to live a life without poverty. This is a satisfactory life but not an affluent life. We do not envisage to create rich persons or communities. On the contrary the Sarvodaya objective is to create a no-poverty society. This is an achievable target as we have experienced so far. So based on the Thought of Awakening of All, Sharing our labour and other resources, we Engage ourselves in a well-thought-out programme of self-development to satisfy Ten Basic Human Needs.

Take the example of the basic need of an access road to a village. The government has not been able to provide the village with a road due to the lack of funds in their budgetary provisions. This is not a priority to the government, but it is a priority for the village community. They cannot wait, because, without a road they cannot take their produce to the market, children could not go to school and a patient could not be taken to hospital for medical care. So they take up this matter, discuss about it and decide to do it by themselves in the spirit of Sarvodaya - 'We build the road and the road builds us.'

Members of the Sarvodaya Shramadana Society of the village divide themselves into groups and undertake to do different tasks preparing for the Shramadana Camp to be conducted during a fixed period. Getting written agreement to donate land from those who own the lands through which the proposed road is to be constructed, actual demarcation of the road, calling for volunteers, collecting the necessary tools and equipment to work, to obtain small machines if needed and available from the local authorities or from those who own them, to prepare accommodation for the night if volunteers from nearby villages come, collection of food, beverages and making other logistical arrangements for cooking etc, to get the services from the staff of the nearby Sarvodaya Divisional and District Centre or the Sarvodaya Head Office depending on the size of the projects and the numbers who will participate, are some of the preparatory tasks to be done.

In a Shramadana Camp usually six to eight hours of manual work for the construction of the road is done per day. At the same time they spend two to four hours or more daily in what are called family gatherings. The purpose of the family gatherings is not only for planning for implementation and evaluation of the projects. It is more for spiritual, moral and cultural awakening of the participants to build a new society. Participants may range in an average camp from a few hundreds to a couple of thousands depending on the work to be done. Quite apart from the manual work done by the participants and their physical achievements by way of the length of road constructed, there are the above mentioned non-material targets to be achieved which are equally or more important.

Camp leaders explain to the participants Codes of Conduct in the camp pertaining to Self-Security, Self-Discipline and Self-Denial. Self-security primarily is concerned with physical care and protection when engaged in manual work, consuming water and food, bathing in rivers and tanks, working in forests and jungles etc. Self-discipline is mostly with regard to inter-personal relationships, abstinence from the popularly accepted five evils, namely, from killing, stealing, sexual misconduct, lying and consuming intoxicating substances, in talking to one another, sharing food, accommodation and other limited facilities when large numbers work together. Self-denial is mostly the cultivation of mental discipline to overcome ego-centricity, idleness, discriminating against age, sex, religious, racial and other differences.

A shramadana camp is like an University of Life where no barriers exist, not even age barriers. In this educational setting all learn from a dual experience - one: lessons learnt from shared labour, feelings, work experience and physical achievements; and two: lessons learnt more or less intuitively - spiritual benefits. Most participants are young people, either still at school or just after school. The inculcation of values such as dignity of physical labour, working with others in a spirit of co-operation and self-sacrifice for the good of others also take place in a camp.

For the individual it is an awakening of his or her personality by consciously as well as involuntarily cultivating the qualities of Loving Kindness towards all (Mettā), Compassionate Actions to remove causes that bring about suffering to people (Karunā), Experiencing the Joy of serving others (Muditā) and Learning to accept both loss and gain, name and blame, success and failure, with detachment and Equanimity (Upekkhā). Buddha called these qualities four sublime abodes.

Similarly in a shared-work situation like this four qualities of group conduct that are necessary for peace and progress are cultivated. These are Beneficence (Dāna), Pleasant Language (Priya Vacana), Constructive Activity (Arthacaryā) and Equality in association (Samanathmantā).

Shramadana Camps are a methodology adopted by Sarvodaya to build a psycho-social infrastructure for all round development of a community. In this key players are the members of the community itself. The inherent strengths and potentialities all human beings have are given an opportunity to flourish for individual and social benefit in this activity. Self-reliance and community participation are promoted. Planning for the achievement of a target they themselves have chosen provides them with experience to undertake bigger tasks.

In addition to gift of labour everyone can donate whatever possessions or skills they possess for the common weal. In a world in which 'possessive individualism' (as Prof. David Kalupahana calls it) seems to dominate over all other altruistic attitudes everyone is given an opportunity to practice giving - 'dana' - rather than acquiring and hoarding wealth and knowledge all the time. A physician helps the sick free of charge - Vaidyādana, a Health Educator imparts knowledge on health care - Saukyadāna, a teacher works on eradication of illiteracy - Buddhidāna, A technical persons gives advice from what he knows - Silpadāna, and religious persons guide the people on spiritual awakening - Dhammadana. Those who can donate money (Dhanadana), material (Sampathdāna) or land (Bhoomidāna) and so on for the project can do so. Sharing thus becomes a commonly accepted social practice.

We are not talking here of national or world economic management which is so distant from a village community whose basic human needs even are not met. The type of economics they need and relevant to them is that which will help them to satisfy their needs. An economic theory however much sophisticated it is, is subservient to the practice of doing something concrete within their own environment that sustains them.

From those practices they build their own economic "theory" supportive of the life they really live and aim to live, unlike professional economists who are employed in national and world economic management systems who devise from time to time ways to maintain economic stability in nations and the world - without a concern for all, ignoring the interdependence of the multitude of factors which condition our lives - resulting in widespread sufferings, frustrations and resentments.

The remedy these economists have for the sufferings, frustrations and resentments of a substantial proportion of humanity, is advocating poverty alleviation and increasingly poverty eradication. The utter inadequacy of their economic theorising is evident from the fact that it is largely the practice of their own theories which has created poverty. There appears to be a very fundamental weakness in theories whose practice produces extreme affluence at one end and extreme poverty at the other. We at Sarvodaya believing firmly in the principles I referred to earlier - a major one being the Respect for All Life - are trying to build a No Poverty/No Affluence society against very severe odds.

A close integration between social and economic objectives is established in the people's consciousness when they participate in a shramadāna camp. No economic policy is worth its name if it does not take into consideration how people will be affected when it is implemented. The economy should serve the people and not the vice versa as it happens today at the macro-economic planning. When a shramadāna is planned specific human needs are identified by the people and satisfaction of those becomes the goal. This is far removed from policies like getting the inflation rate down or getting rid of subsidies and restrictions to allow free play of market forces.

Lecture Five:
Building a No-Poverty Society

The Economic Objective of Sarvodaya, if it can be said so, is a No-Poverty Society. Sarvodaya rejects the goal of Affluence for All for very practical reasons. Affluence cannot be achieved by all. It cannot be reached easily without using wrong means. A country or the world simply does not have resources to provide affluence for all. Social, environmental, moral and cultural costs of trying to build an affluent society are very heavy. It generally increases the already existing gap between the poor and the rich. An affluent person or society is not necessarily happier than a non-poor person or society.

The best way to measure the progress of a community is to find out at what level the poorest people live. If they can be in a state of no-poverty that can be our starting point for so-called development.

How do we define no-poverty society for the purposes of designing and implementing our programs in village communities?

Sarvodaya enables the people to find out the level to which Basic Human Needs of a person, a family or a community is satisfied so that there is no poverty. What are the Basic Human Needs as accepted by Sarvodaya? They are:

1. A Clean and Beautiful Environment (Both physical and psychological)
2. A Clean and Adequate supply of Water
3. Minimum Requirements of Clothing
4. Balanced Food Requirements
5. A Simple House to live in
6. Basic Health Care
7. Simple Communication Facilities
8. Minimum Energy requirements
9. Total Education
10. Cultural and Spiritual Needs

Without these minimum requirements being fulfilled it is difficult for a householder to devote time wholeheartedly for spiritual development. According to different times and climes, and other factors, these Ten Basic Human Needs, when subdivided into subneeds may take different forms. There can be as many as 180 subneeds. For example in a cold climate the clothing or housing requirements may be quite different from that of a tropical place. In Sarvodaya work, members of communities have decided upon sometimes from 15 to 20 subneeds under each basic human need. The rationale behind the analysis of these basic human needs is the status of the weakest population group in a community and the objective of improving their level of living.

Employment is not considered by Sarvodaya as a basic human need. Employment brings income for a person, which is used to buy what is required to satisfy the needs. So employment and income are means of satisfying needs and are not needs by themselves. Thus in Sarvodaya 'income' and 'employment' are not central and have only a limited relevance, especially during the initial stages. The aim of production in a village economy is not to accumulate profit but satisfy the needs of the local community. The criterion Sarvodaya uses is not a speculative exchange value in an unknown market. It is a real use value in their own households.

On the other hand Sarvodaya places great importance in the engagement of every member of the community in processes that play a role in basic need satisfaction. This provides them an opportunity to be industrious, to co-operate for common benefit, learn skills and understand problems and exercise their minds to seek solutions.

Poverty does not exist in isolation. Related to poverty, ignorance, disease, stagnation, oppression and so on co-exist. It is a vicious cycle. What causes this vicious cycle also is a number of interrelated factors. If we are to break this vicious cycle a Cycle of Hope has to be released. This has to be followed by a practical Way. This way of analysis is modeled after Buddha's Four Noble Truths; There is Suffering (Dukkha), There is a Cause to this suffering (Samudaya), This Cause can be Removed (Nirodha), and There is Way (Magga) of doing this. Graphically this model can be shown as follows:

If the cause of decadence start with egosim, possession, competition and so on then to release their opposite forces of non-egoism, non-possession, co-operation and so on correct conditions have to be created for people to participate and work. This is exactly what a shramadana camp does and it was briefly described during the last lecture.

PATH TO VILLAGE RE-AWAKENING
GRAMODAYA

DECENT VILLAGE   THERE IS A CAUSE   THERE IS A HOPE   THERE IS A WAY

This type of participation brings about hope in the form of egolessness, equality, constructive engagement, pleasant speech and so on opening a new Path to Awaken.

The Path has many interrelated and interdependent components such as a Vision as expressed by the Sarvodaya Philosophy, a Mission to which people are psychologically bound and are dedicated, Goals and Objectives determining various actions, and Organizational forms facilitating planning, implementation, management and so on. All these are directed to bring about an awakening in the fields of Educational, Health, Cultural, Moral and Spiritual life of people.

The optimum number of families in a village community, that Sarvodaya finds it easier to organize, is between 100 to 150. It is best that the villages where there are more than 200 families are organized into two or more sub-villages or 'gamgodas'. Through shramadāna camps initial psycho-social infra-structure building is progressively achieved by the village communities. Villagers themselves select one or more of their felt-needs and with their own self-reliance and community participation these needs are satisfied.

To begin with, the social (organizational) infrastructure in a village, consists of various formations such as the pre-school age children, compulsory school-going age children, out of school youth between the ages 16-26, mothers, adults, farmers and so on. Each formation is related to certain activities which fall within the agenda of basic human needs. This is a stage in village development wherein leadership skills get developed, community leadership potential is discovered, training in vocational skills is given and in general the problems are identified and solutions are sought by the people themselves.

The various social formations in a village really come of age when the village as a whole is ready to get incorporated as an incorporated body under the accepted governmental laws. Such a legal entity is called Village Sarvodaya Shramadana Society. It is this orgnaization from then onwards that plays the leading role of awakening the village in all aspects, namely, social, economic and political, as well as spiritual, moral and cultural.

THE SOCIAL INFRASTRUCTURE IN A SARVODAYA VILLAGE

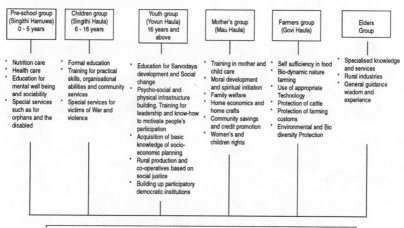

Pre-school group (Singithi Hamuwa) 0 - 5 years	Children group (Singithi Haula) 6 - 16 years	Youth group (Yovun Haula) 16 years and above	Mother's group (Mau Haula)	Farmers group (Govi Haula)	Elders Group
* Nutrition care * Health care * Education for mental well being and sociability * Special services such as for orphans and the disabled	* Formal education * Training for practical skills, organisational abilities and community services * Special services for victims of War and violence	* Education for Sarvodaya development and Social change * Psycho-social and physical infrastructure building. Training for leadership and know-how to motivate people's participation * Acquisition of basic knowledge of socio-economic planning * Rural production and co-operatives based on social justice * Building up participatory democratic institutions	* Training in mother and child care * Moral development and spiritual initiation * Family welfare * Home economics and home crafts * Community savings and credit promotion * Women's and children rights	* Self sufficiency in food * Bio-dynamic nature farming * Use of appropriate Technology * Protection of cattle * Protection of farming customs * Environmental and Bio diversity Protection	Specialised knowledge and services * Rural industries * General guidance wisdom and experience

VILLAGE SARVODAYA SHRAMADANA SOCIETY

VILLAGE SARVODAYA
SHRAMADANA SOCIETY: ORGANIZATION CHART

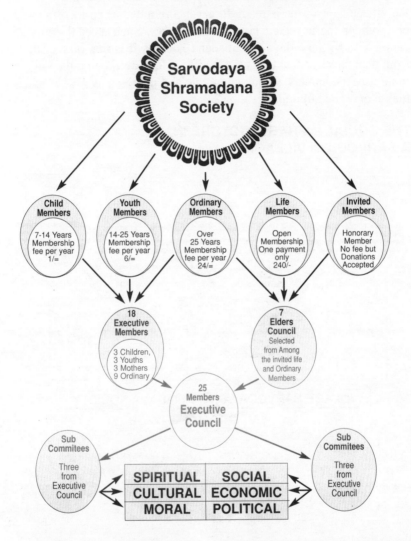

In the kind of participastory approach to development that Sarvodaya practices so many processes converge on the realization of personal and social awakening. Changes in the thinking of people and
their attitudes, innovation of methods, techniques and technologies in

the execution of basic human needs satisfaction programmes, and, evolution and institutionalization of appropriate structures within democratic control of basic communities, are three such sectors that converge harmoniously in this self-development exercise of the people.

All Village Sarvodaya Shramadāna Societies are governed by a set of Rules, which the members accept and ratify at the inaugural General Meeting itself. Competent lawyers subject to the prevailing Constitution of Sri Lanka and other Laws of the country formulated these rules. These societies when recognized and registered by the Registrar of Societies / Companies have full autonomy to operate as independent legal entities. Today nearly 3000 village societies out of the 11600 villages where Sarvodaya is active have their own registered societies. Others will soon follow.

Their General Principles (Rule 7) are similar to those of the Sarvodaya Shramadana Movement of Sri Lanka which is the principal national Sarvodaya body incorporated by an Act of Parilament (No. 12 of 1972). However the General Objects (Rule 6) cover not only all matters pertaining to basic need satisfaction and village development but also those sectors pertaining to co-ordination with local and central government services, other voluntary and private bodies, industrial, trade and financial matters, but also using even foreign markets to the advantage of rural communities.

Over the years Sarvodaya has forumulated a five-stage process of Village Development.

Stage 1: Sarvodaya Shramadana Camps in which both villagers from the village itself and other Sarvodaya volunteers from neighbouring villages participate to provide the village with essential services as roads, latrines, wells, tank bunds, irrigation canals, reforestation programmes etc with emphasis on mutual benefit to the community.

Stage 2: Formation of peer groups such as mothers' groups, children's groups, youth groups, farmers' groups and so on and provision of training for them in leadership on child-care, health and sanitation etc so that they can effectively participate in basic needs satisfaction programmes.

Stage 3: Through self-reliance and community participation satisfaction of basic needs in the village and the formation of a village level Sarvodaya Shramadana Society registered under government regulations capable of giving organized leadership to all village level activities that lead to the improvement of their standard of living.

Stage 4: Introduction of Sarvodaya Economic Enterprises Development Services to the village and progressively developing the capacity of the villagers to save, to borrow, to improve the existing enterprises, to start new ones, to repay the loans and evolve their own village development bank.

Stage 5: Building economic relationships with the neighbouring villages, strengthening the capacity in money, products and services so that the latter too could become a part of a cluster of villages along with other clusters of villages in the country contributing to the building of an alternative approach to economic development where the rural areas are benefited.

Sarvodaya is not a growth oriented development as far as growth is dependent on non-renewable resources. Yet economic growth is essential and it has to take place with due acceptance of the rights of all forms of life for the resources of the planet, promoting equal and non-exploitative relationships between human beings and recognizing interdependence between human beings, the society and nature. This is not an easy task. But the Five-Stage development process that Sarvodaya practices facilitates what may be even be called Sustainable Development.

You may realize from whatever I have described so far that the Sarvodaya approach to development is a very pragmatic one starting with what people know they need, and, trying to satisfy those with what they have both in respect of material resources and know-how. Whatever outside help that comes supplements their own efforts. This approach is different from both the western capitalistic enconomics and Marxist economics. Sarvodaya not only recognizes that people have basic material needs that have to be satisfied to overcome poverty but also that the methods applied in implementing the poverty-eradication programmes should also not violate the norms that are held in high esteem by the people. The ethical values and right conduct are necessary to satisfy their spiritual aspirations. The methodology that Sarvodaya has developed over a period of four decades is, in fact, an attempt to bring about a balance between these two conflicting approaches.

The prevalent economic theories of both the western and Marxist brands are well developed, documented and have been praticed over a long period of time. An approach like that of Sarvodaya has a long way to go before it can build up a clear economic theory and practice which one may call Buddhist Economics. Even building up a distinct terminology to clearly express what we mean and make it intelligible to others is a time-consuming task. So we have to use the existing economic language and even the current divisions such as micro-economics, macro-economics and specialized subjects like public finance in our work also. We have also to operate and do our work within the existing laws of the country and the administrative and financial frameworks. When it comes to statistical computations and measurables we are at a great disadvantage when compared with those of the traditional current econometricians as our tools have yet to be developed. In spite of these constraints the Sarvodaya Shramadana Movement is striving to build a working model. What was described so far is the foundation of such a model.

For example Sarvodaya does not consider the classical factors of production such as Land, Labour, Capital and Entrepreneurship as those that have to be used merely to create wealth. We look at these and other related resources as important for the survival, sustainability and wellbeing of not only our generation but also future generations and the other living beings and nature itself. Therefore, when Sarvodaya gets into economic activities, issues such as profits, speculation, hoarding, competitiveness, shares and stock markets and so on become of secondary importance. The main concern is satisfaction of basic needs, secondary needs and tertiary needs, in that order, through Right Livelihood in a Full-Engagement Society.

The concerns of governments, private sector bodies and international political and economic instutitions are different. They are not concerned with the awakening of all. They are guided by concepts of globalization, market economies, full-employment, sustainable growth and so on. However these are the leading forces in societies and even a movement for radical non-violent social change such as Sarvodaya has to act within the limitations imposed by them. It is in this context that we have to devise ways and means, innovate methods and technologies, and build new institutions to coexist with them without getting co-opted, to carry on with our programmes.

Sarvodaya Early Childhood Development Programme, Sarvodaya Women's Movement, Sarvodaya Legal Services Movement, Sarvodaya Peace Brigades Movement, Sarvodaya Rural Technical Services, Sarvodaya Economic Enterprises Development Services, Sarvodaya Community Health Services, Sarvodaya Bio-diversity and Environmental Conservation Programme and Sarvodaya Suwa Setha Services Society are such innovative institutions and programmes all of which merge together at the level of the village to build the alternative society. The village movement itself, which has now 11600 villages at different stages of the five-stage development scheme, is aimed at Grām Swarājya or village self-government.

Each village strives to satisfy their basic needs. Then a cluster of ten villages come together to satisfy their secondary needs. Then several clusters at divisional, district and national levels strive to influence the local, provincial and central governments in policies and decisions that would ultimately satisfy their secondary and tertiary needs. So the task of Sarvodaya is two-fold. It has to go on with its poverty eradica-

The Law of Diminishing Returns and Buddhist Equilibrium

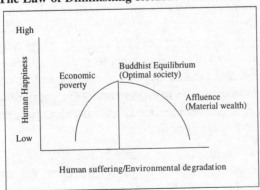

Source:
Patrick Mendis (1993),
Buddhist Equilibrium:
The Middle Path for Human
Happiness and
Environmental
Sustainability.
(St. Paul: University of
Minnesota Department of
Applied Economics

tion programmes on one hand and on the other hand develop a conceptual as well as a methodical - institutional framework in the light of practical experience. This entails an educational programme aimed not only at the village communities but also at those who wield political and administrative powers at divisional, district, provincial and national levels. Establishment of correct rapport with persons and institutions at all these levels has to be done at all times.

Lecture Six:
Replacing Full-Employment with Full-Engagement - Right Livelihood

The whole world seems to be obsessed with the idea that after a particular age every Human being should be employed in a paid job. This also implies that the period before such employment is one where the human being is prepared by the society to take up such employment. So the entire educational system and what is known as human development are principally geared to this task even though other objectives such as moulding of character are also mentioned.

The entire Western Economics appears to have been geared to an objective, known as full employment, which has not been fully realized in practice anywhere. It also appears that if by some magic full employment is realized the entire Western economic system may collapse. In so-called developing countries also which have adopted this idea the same objective is pursued without being able to realize in practice even to the extent the rich countries have achieved.

The political, economic, and social structures including the subtle but very strong coercive institutions have protected the rich societies from internal social upheavals due to problems arising from unemployment and underemployment. On the other hand, in poorer countries internal social upheavals have taken bloody revolutionary proportions using most sophisticated conventional weapons produced in rich countries where the armament industry is one of the biggest employment generating economic enterprises.

From the experience we have gained from the Sarvodaya approach to development we believe that for all societies but specially the poorer societies, an alternative objective can be kept before their mind which is different from full-employment. We call it the creation of a Right Livelihood Society or a Full-Engagement Society. We know that this objective has to be pursued not in a vacuum but in real life situations where the minds of almost all the people are conditioned to earn money in a society oriented to employment generation. Furthermore, as far as Sarvodaya is concerned, it has to be done without violating ethical values which are held in high esteem by people.

The Concept of Right Livelihood - A Brief Outline

Life has many demands which conventional economics ignores. Such "demands" are also met which is again ignored by the currrent economics. It would be a very rare "economist" who would live without love and affection. If such love and affection were not shown at his/her birth and during the helpless infancy, he/she may not have survived to expound the "economics". The very survival of the human race depends on such love and affection among other factors. But there is no "production function" in economic theory which accounts for such "produce". Right livelihood is concerned with such considerations affecting the life of ALL on earth.

Central to the concept of Right livelihood as being expounded in this lecture, is the notion of the engagement of each and every individual in socially acceptable and useful activities (constructive activitries) which also give them a sense of satisfaction. An individual may not be "employed" in the economic sense but may be and could frequently be engaged in socially acceptable and useful activities.

Even little children could be so engaged. They also delight in being so engaged. Apart from the well-known fact of children helping with the household chores, special activities could be organized where children have a specific and very useful role to play. A major community development activity of Sarvodaya is the Shramadana Camp in which the bulk of the physical work such as repairing a road or irrigation channel or digging a well is done by the youth and the elders. The children carry the water and food to the workers and are also the messengers. They also learn by observing their elders at work. They also learn to work together for the common good. They participate in the traditional cultural activities which are often associated with such work in a community. In fact during breaks in the work, children may be either singing songs or performing a dance providing part of the common entertainment and may themselves watch performances by the elders. Apart from providing a useful service children do learn. Many other examples could be given of such services by children.

The above example also indicates constructive work by youth and elders. Such work has economic worth. The construction of roads, houses, wells, latrines, pre-schools, community halls etc. by communities in such organized manner is not reflected in the GDP. But they certainly contribute to improving the quality of life in the rural and urban deprived communities. Such work could be organized in the more affluent communities as well although the nature of the work may be different. For example much of the work in urban areas may be about keeping the environment clean, cultural activities and the like.

At the level of youth and adults, such engagements also involve skill training and acquiring certain technical knowledge as well. Skill training may be in such traditional areas as carpentry and masonry. Of late technical knowledge and skills in relation to water supply, sewage disposal and solar power are provided. Such constructive work by youth and adults also lead to employment in the traditional economic sense. The community may collectively pay the skilled workmen. There also may be the individual needs to be met of those who could pay for the services. For those who cannot pay, the community as a whole may meet the cost of the services.

Right Livelihood does not ignore the elders in a community. They also have a role to play. Generally they are the repositories of the collective community wisdom and any community activity is generally discussed with them and initiated and conducted with thier advice and blessing. They are not discarded as being "economically inactive" and being only a burden on the economically active. Elders have a definite leadership role to play. They are not "senior citizens" confined to homes for elders and outside the mainstream of life in the community.

Right Livelihood also accords an important place for the spirirual needs of the community. A community may accord greater importance for the construction of a place of religious worship than for the construction of a well or a road. In the conventional economic view that may not be an investment. But communities in fact make such decisions even now. Such constructions and services are not included in the GDP. But they provide a great deal of satisfaction for the people. Such activities contribute to building up of a psychological infrastructure in the community. Communities will make "optimal allocation of resources" in terms of their concept of right livelihood. The time frame for their "objective function" may well be beyond this life.

There is no wastage of human resources, frustration and other such accompaniments of the "unemployment" which appear inevitable under the current economic thinking and practice.

Application of Right Livelihood in a community

During a period close upon four decades, the Sarvodaya Movement has used the concept of right livelihood in its work in Sri Lankan communities in all parts of the country representative of all ethnic and religious groups. The essence of the concept is the engagement of ALL in constructive activities. A major reason for Sarvodaya being able to do so is that in spite of the many changes affecting the life of the people, the large majority of the communities still hold on to the traditional values.

It is the Sarvodaya experience that doing something good irrespective of monetary considerations is still a valued principle in life for most people particularly in the rural community and among the urban poor. Sarvodaya through its practical community development activities has made it possible for people to practice this principle and demonstrate that it is still valid even when "money" reigns supreme. The flickering flame that Sarvodaya has so far kept alive, it may no longer be able to protect, let alone provide for its spreading.

Sarvodaya works in around 11,400 communities in all parts of the country including the North and the East and representing all the major ethnic and religious groups. It has developed a local-level leadership borne of each community which is capable of continuing this development work. It has also developed a wide-spread organisational structure, based on three main Divisions, namely, the Social Empowerment Division, the Technical Empowerment Division and the Economic Empowerment Division, to support this leadership. The initial building up of the psycho-social infrastructure of the community, providing for the acquisition of leadership skills for the social empowerment of the community and for the acquisition of the technical knowledge and skills for the technical and economic empowerment of the community are what these services accomplish. The various programmes under these Divisions have been operating successfully.

At the community level, the demonstrated Sarvodaya practices, indicate a development path, which has the potential to resolve the many problems for which current economic thinking and practices have neither theoretical nor practical solutions.

In Sarvodaya thinking, employment as such is not a basic human need. Employment is to produce some goods or service to meet a basic human need. The operation of the free market does not lead to the meeting of the basic human needs of the community such as a clean environment, clean drinking water, reasonable housing, adequate food,....This is a fact, unpleasant though it may be. The communities are on the whole too poor economically, though not otherwise, to convert their needs into "demands" which may be met by "supplies". Owners of capital can maximize their objective functions without trying to meet the basic human need of the poor. In fact under current economic practices they simply will go bankrupt if they try to meet these basic human needs.

Sarvodaya has demonstrated that the full engagement of ALL in the community can lead to the satisfaction of basic human needs even in the absence of "full employment" as economists conceive. Sarvodaya does not envisage that there will be no "employment". While a certain segment of the community, according to the capacity of the economy, is employed in agricultural, agro-industrial, industrial and other similar activities related to production and distribution, the rest of the community may be gainfully engaged in those constructive activities contributing to the improvement of their quality of life. To expand on the brief references made earlier, this may occur in a community as follows:

Early childhood - Children under 5 years

The nutrition, health, educational and psycho-social needs of these children have to be met. The state does provide some services which do not reach many. The state provides no educational service for this group. Under Sarvodaya leadership, several thousand communities now have "Child-care-centres" constructed and maintained by the community itself. Several thousand young women, trianed by Sarvodaya, render completely voluntary services while

- 44 -

some others are paid a small allowance by their respective communities.

These workers at community level are guided by trained Sarvodaya staff. Trained Sarvodaya staff also conduct training classes for mothers on child and maternal nutrition in selected villages, the restriction being the availability of funds.

Though under 5 years of age, these children are not only recievers of a service. In their own way and within their own physical and other limitations, they also render certain services. As mentioned earlier they participate in running their own centres, shramadana activities, cleaning places of religious worship, etc.

Mid-childhood - Children from 5 - about 16 years

The state provides a formal school and in Sri Lanka the access is good with nearly all such children attendintg school. There is non-enrollment and dropouts but the percentages are small. How may these children be engaged in constructive activities?

Sarvodaya has organised such children into Groups and they are among the most active groups in communities. They also take part in shramadana activities and in cultural and religious activities which are an important part of community life. Libraries are also being organised for their benefit. Home gardening, week-end children's fair and children's savings programmes are also important activities they are engaged in.

The older children and some of the youth are organized as groups which engage in providing such services as primary health care for the community, visits to hospitals to provide some solace to the sick, providing first aid at community/national festivals, maintaining herbal gardens, protecting the bio-diversity, engaging in social forestry and generally taking care of the environment, etc. Another important area of work relates to conflict resolution and establishment of peace and harmony through well-triained Peace Brigades. These groups are provided with some formal training to engage in their various activities.

Youth - Males/females from about 16 - 26 years

The population in this age group, comprising both those in and out of school are organised into Youth Groups. The Youth Groups comprise the main source of labour in the shramadana camps and thus contribute in great measure to the physical infrastructure development in the community.

Where this age group is concerned vocational training courses are organised with a view to obtaining employment. The training, however, is geared to meeting basic human needs. Increasinghly training is being provided in such areas as solar panel installations, maintenance of gravity-fed water supply schemes, use of computers, preventing environmental degradation and conservation of biodiversity, non-violent conflict resolution, human rights and duties.

Mothers' Group

The mothers' group is for females and is the most prevalent and active of the various groups Sarvodaya has attempted to generate in communities. Their main concern is with children and lactating and pregnant mothers. The Child-care Centre in the community is managed by the Mothers' Group. It is being converted into a Development Centre for the community. Even at present, it serves not only the children but the lactating and pregnant mothers and the elderly by providing them with meals, health education and nutritional-know-how.

Increasingly the Mothers' Group is being utilized by the Sarvodaya Women's Movement (an independent organisation with its own charter) as a vehicle for improving the condition of women and addressing gender issues. Small loans for economic activities are being channelled through these groups.

Occupational Groups

These comprise principally farmers. The economic activities they are engaged in are supported through training programmes and credit facilities. Groups also make collective purchases to reduce cost of inputs. Technical advice is given regarding storage of agicultural produce so that post-harvest losses can be reduced and better prices may be obtained. Providing market information is another such service. Members are also encouraged to "add value'" to their produce through training programmes, seminars and literature.

The Village Society

The various groups referred to above provide for any one in the community to engage in a constructive activity depending on his/her age, ability and inclination. The formal Sarvodaya organisation encourages and supports such activities. A very important consideration is that such activities are chosen by the communities and are not imposed on them.

The planning and coordination of these activities and further development of the community have led to the creation of village societies registered under the law. They are legal entities with well-defined rights and obligations. The training of the office-bearers of these societies is another major service rendered by the Sarvodaya organisation.

Well-developed societies have their own credit fund, are able to obtain loans from banks on commercial rates, manage their own loan fund, grant loans to its members and are in fact capable of helping neighbouring communities. The interest from the loans has in some cases been enough to maintain a pre-school teacher for the community in addition to maintaining a credit fund manager from the community.

A more recent development has been the creation of Village Development Banks in collaboration with commercial banks and a loan scheme with a leading state sector bank.

The brief description given above indicates that Sarvodaya practices enable all people in a community to be not only usefully engaged but also contribute to the development of the village economy in a very substantial way. **It is a system which while operating within the current economic practices indicates a way of overcoming the many disadvantages the urban and rural poor suffer under the current economic policies.**

Lecture Seven:
Impact of "Employment" on the Sarvodaya Sangamaya itself - Sustainability of Sarvodaya Development Processes

The Continuing Dilemma of "Employment"

The last two decades have seen some remakable changes in the world. A very major one was the collapse of the "command economies" and accompanying it the proliferation of the "open economy" and "free market policies." Globalization is presented as the panacea for all our ills. There is now hardly any elite in any country in the world who do not subscribe to these economic policies. Markets now apparently have no national frontiers to contend with. Trade barriers are being dismantled to permit free flow of goods although at the moment, goods are "more free" to move from North to South than in the other direction. It is expected that in the future there would be a free flow of not only goods but of services as well. At present there are many restrictions to the flow of services from South to North.

Another major change is the change in attitude to the environment and the inclusion of "environmental costs" in economic considerations. The traditional factors of production are no longer adequate for economic decisions. This is not entirely due to a change of heart by the "owners of capital". It is due to public pressure arising from the concern for environment at global, macro and micro levels.

The new information technology has transformed micro groups into a very powerful mass movement. Nowhere in the world is it possible now to start any large-scale economic enterprise without environmental consideration being addressed. Even if the people immediately affected are not able to protest either through ignorance/apathy, there are other groups which will bring up the issues. The balance between the usual economic activities on the one hand and the sustenance of the environment on the other are matters of lively debate. In many instances the "environmentalists" have won the day and have managed to stall if not altogether stop some economic activities. Economists now have another factor to contend with.

The last two decades have also seen an increasing recognition of the contribution by women to the economy. Although their contribution is still to be reflected in such standard and widely used indicators as the GNP, it is now accepted that any such indicators which ignore the contribution of women are not adequate. Attempts are being made to cost the work done by women not only in the household but in agriculture and in the informal sector.

In spite of these changes which are rapidly affecting the way people think and live, there is one aspect which has remained virtually unchanged, namely, the question of "employment". Whatever economic system a country has had or is in the process of trying to establish, the one common element has been the question of "employment". The ILO Report on "World Employment 1995" describes the situation in the following terms.

Anxiety over employment problems as well as pessimism over the prospects for resolving them reign in many parts of the world today. Indeed the task of creating sufficient new jobs to overcome unemployment, underemployment and problems of low pay ranks as the primary challenge for economic and social policy in countries at all levels of development across the globe. The reason why this is so is easy enough to understand. High levels of unemployment spawn a host of problems: growing inequality and social exclusion, the waste of foregone output and unutilized human resources; increasing economic insecurity, and the human suffering inflicted on the unemployed. In contrast, a high and stable rate of productive job creation is the mainspring of equitable economic and social development.

The ILO Report is hopeful. It believes that steps such as the following would resolve the problem:

- A universal commitment to the goal of full employment.
- Place the employment issue at the centre of the international agenda, resulting in,

  Cooperative international action to reduce social tensions and make policies more effective;

  More equitable sharing of the costs and benefits of globalization.

There is no government which is not committed to "full-employment". At least at the level of rhetoric there is no national political leader who is not so committed. There is no election manifesto which fails to provide "more employment." With the end of the command economies, democratic elections are more and more the order of the day.

Some but not much faith may be put on "international cooperative action". Alleviation of poverty has been on the international agenda for more than a decade. Poverty is increasing. The eradication of illiteracy was on UNESCO's agenda at its birth. UNESCO has celebrated its 50th Anniversary with the world having more illiterates than ever before in its history.

The reduction of the arms race between the super powers is a success story clouded by the continuing development of destructive explosive nuclear devices by some countries. A notable gain has been the eradication of small-pox. Peace on earth is still a distant dream. People on earth still die of starvation.

"Equitable sharing" is not consistent with the "open economy" and "free trade". Free competition, supply and demand are the forces which govern the economy at whatever level. "Sharing" is not in the economic vocabulary other than in the sense of "purchasing one's share". If you do not have what it takes to purchase your share you just do not get it. People do not die of starvation for lack of food. They die of starvation because they do not have the purchasing power. Some people having puchasing power and some not having puchasing power is again an inevitable concomitant of the "open economy".

Supply and demand also imply a "supply of labour". It is the cheap labour in the developing countries which has led to the starting of much industrial activity in them. Industrial or economic activity shifts according to, among other factors, the cost for labour. It is in the interest of the "owners of capital" to see to it that there is always a pool of labour to recruit from. It is in their interests to increase the pool and not to decrease the pool. The free play of economic forces postulates a point of equilibrium between supply and demand and thus theoretically there should be unemployment.

It appears, therefore, that despite the optimism of the ILO, the "employment problem" is going to be a continuing one unless there is some thinking not just about economics but about life on earth in its fullest sense. Life is governed by other considerations besides, "optional allocation of resources" and "maximizing the objective function".

Sarvodaya "employees"

After four decades of work on the lines of a full-engagement society with many thousands of communities successfully it appeared to us that Sarvodaya's very succecss brought with it the seeds of its own downfall. Sarvodaya was in many a sense fortunate, but in another unfortunate to attract the attention and support of the international donor agencies. The largely volunteer staff of the earlier decades came to be replaced by larger numbers of more qualified and paid staff many of whom regarded Sarvodaya as just another employer. The improvement of the quality of its services was accompanied by escalating maintenance costs for which also Sarvodaya had to rely on increasingly reluctant donors. Donors had their own agendas and targets set by donors came to replace the decisions made by communities. Sarvodaya lost its freedom to act. Development came to be regarded as a target to be met and not a process to be initiated and sustained. Purely economic criteria, limited as I have shown them to be, came to be applied to the Sarvodaya work.

On hindsight Sarvodaya has come to the conclusion that what Sarvodaya is attempting do is understood best by the communities themselves because the ideas and practices arose from them. Sarvodaya philosophy and practice are not an invention of the Sarvodaya Sangamaya but a distillation of the essence of community thinking and practice. There is no Sarvodaya practice which has not had its origin in some community initiative.

Getting out of "employment" and into "Right Livelihood" for Sarvodaya staff

The Sarvodaya experience has shown that with a minimum support communities will progress on the path they have chosen. It has also shown that communities may and do help each other. In developing a new strategy to continue with its development work without succumbing to extraneous influences, Sarvodaya is concentrating its efforts on a selected set of villages who will in turn provide certain services to neighbouring communities which were earlier provided by the Sarvodaya Sangamaya itself. These are the Pioneering Villages and as of now Sarvodaya has identified around 1100 such villages. Each Pioneering Village will provide certain services to 4 other villages in this vicinity. The group of 5 villages thus working together will in turn influence 5 other villages in their vicinity, leading to a total of 10 villages around a Pioneering Village. It will thus be possible to influence a total of around 11,000 villages.

The minimum support to be extended to these Pioneering Villages consists of certain material and financial inputs which the community should directly receive and other services, primarily trianing which they may receive either through Sarvodaya or through other agencies either in the public and/or private sector.

More specifically societies in Pioneering Villages need to be supported primarily in two ways.

One is to support them to consolidate their structure, train their leaders and acquire the necessary technical and economic knowledge and skills to provide for every one in the community to be engaged in constructive economic activities. Such institutional support may be extended in the form of an outright grant to the village society which is empowered under the law to receive and be accountable for such grants. The village society will utilize the income from the grant to improve the village physical infrastructure, attend to environmental conservation, take steps to conserve the bio-diversity and train village leaders, students, etc. in these areas using modern technology. Accordingly, the grant may be also be utilized to improve the existing working spaces and provide for such modern communication equipment as a telephone, a fax machine and a computer and associated equipment. It may also provide for the employment of two full-time workers for a period of two years until they can be supported by the income of the village society. The village society will also utilize the village elders, religious leaders and the learned people to build up the social infrastructure and the cultural identity of the village.

The second way is to give a loan to the society to engage in conventional economic activities. This loan will be utilized by the Village Development Bank while the grant will be received by the village society. The Village Development Bank will pay commercial interest to the village society for the grant desposited with the Bank while the interest on the loan granted will be paid to the donor after a grace period.

To support this whole development effort the Sarvodaya Sangamaya has to have a annual outright income to maintain its national, district and divisional centres so that service may continue to be rendered by them to the selected village societies in the progressive way described above. For this purpose Sarvodaya has started building an Endowment Fund.

This lecture has dealt with the application of the concept of right livelihood at the community level. Sarvodaya is strongly of the belief that the concept is applicable at sub-national, nationl, regional and global levels as well. Even in its present work in communities, there is the attempt to establish cooperative and co-ordinated action between communities in the same vicinity. These may be extended to wider groups which while not being in the vicinity of each other are bound by ties of affinity to create a full-engagement society. Sarvodaya believes that it is well worth pursuing such efforts.

Lecture Eight:
Sarvodaya Economic Enterprises Development Services - Globalization with a Humane Approach

Sarvodaya Economic Enterprises Development Services or SEEDS is the legally independent institutional framework we have developed to extend the concept of right livelihood society or full-engagement society from the grassroots to a national and global level. SEEDS was initiated in 1986 with about 250 village societies in five districts and by the end of 1997 it has extended to nearly 3,000 villages in 18 districts.

The target group of this programme is the multitude of rural poor who are members of the Sarvodaya Shramadana societies. Through the strengthening of village based institutions, finances, assessment of enterprises and capacity building among Sarvodaya Shramadana Society office bearers and members, SEEDS plans to uplift the economic status of the target groups. Although the services were at first limited to institutional strengthening, entrepreneurship training as well as credit services, since 1990 they have been expanded to include business development, agricultural extension services and business information.

SEEDS also permits environment friendly economic development activities and encourages the conservation of the prevailing life styles and values.

To achieve the eradication of poverty among the rural power in Sri Lanka SEEDS has planned to:

- Enhance and stabilize the economic condition and income level of the membership of the Sarvodaya Shramadāna Society (SSS).
- Strengthen each SSS to become a self-reliant, self-funding, self-managing basic institution of village level rural development.
- Ensure the sustainable extension of SEEDS as an alternative development institution.

SEED's integrated approach to economic development consists of three main divisions:

Rural Enterprises Programme (REP) - developer of a people-centered village banking system

- Provision of capital resources for rural development.
- Intensification of rural investment potentials and establishment of special funds by inducing Sarvodaya Shramadāna Society members to increase savings.
- Strengthening of Sarvodaya Shramadāna Societies to play a pivotal role in development.

Management Training Institute (MTI)

(Trainers in management and entrepreneurship development)

- Entrepreneurship development training for low-income and unemployed members.
- Improvement of management knowledge and skills of Sarvodaya Shramadana Society office-bearers.
- Providing community management and leadership training.
- Training of employees of SEEDS and similar organisations.

Rural Enterprises Development Services (REDS)

(Provider of advisory and consultancy services, technical training and information for rural economic development)

- Motivating counselling and providing consultancy services for income generation among Sarvodaya Society Members.
- Providing small business and agriculture extension services.
- Providing technical skills training.
- Research into new options for agriculture and small business development.
- Organizing marketing facilities, building market linkages.
- Collection and dissemination of information pertaining to economic development.

Based on the above organizational structure SEEDS development strategy can be categorized into the following firve forms of activities.

Strengthening of Sarvodaya Shramadāna Societies for economic programmes:

- Organizing peer groups
- Organizing small groups
- Formation of economic sub-committees
- Training of group leaders
- Training of office-bearers of Societies
- Developing management skills
- Developing book-keeping, accounting and financial skills
- Facilitating banking transactions

Orientation of membership for economic development activities:

- Preparation of a development plan for the village
- Develop and induce thrift and savings habits in the membership
- Implementation of short-term loan programmes
- Creation of a favourable credit culture
- Direction of the rural community towards income generating projects.

Development of self-employment and small enterprise projects

- Creation of business awareness and motivation among rural communities
- Assisting members to select suitable enterprises
- Providing training for entrepreneurship development
- Providing training in technology
- Guidance in project planning to the membership
- Undertaking feasibility studies of proposed projects
- Credit facilities for capital investment
- Business consultancy and adivosry services
- Building market linkages

Agriculture development

- Promotion of agriculture as a profit-making enterprise
- Providing training for village-level agricultural volunteers
- Agricultural demonstrations
- Introduction of new crops and crop varieties
- Introduction of agricultural enterprises
- Storage methods for agricultural products
- Development of animal husbandry projects
- Credit facilities for capital investments
- Building market linkages

Poverty Eradication

- Ensuring a better standard of living for SSS members
- Creating more employment and self-employment opportunities for youth and women
- Promoting environment friendly rural economic enterprises

Lastly, if Sarvodaya succeeds in implementing this strategy, the following results can be expected for the future:

- Development of self-managed and financially viable Sarvodaya Shramadāna Societies in more villages.
- Enhancement of rural funding through increased savings.
- Creation of a Rural Banking System through the Sarvodaya Shramadāna Society Savings and Credit Units thereby making an innovative change in the banking sector of Sri Lanka.
- Decentralization of SEEDS on a district basis and building up of a national level team of specialists competent in alternative development methodologies.
- Qualitative and quantitative improvement of self-employment and small-scale enterprises in the villages.
- Reinforcement of entrepreneurship skills to overcome the imbalance in the rural economy created by over-dependence on agriculture.

- Lessening of social injustice through gender education.
- Increasing the participation and decision-making by women in rural economic activities.
- Minimizing youth unrest arising out of unemployment.

This brief description of SEEDS that I have given may have created the impression in your minds that SEEDS is just another economic enterprise on different from many others. The description of our work in currernt terminology makes it very difficult to illustrate the very different approach that we are adopting. I list below some characteristics of our work which is in keeping with the principles I have already referred to:

SEEDS is not trying to create a "rich few". It develops the society as a whole.

It is not destroying the enviornment to make a 'profit'. It neither funds or encourages economic activities which may have udesirable impacts on the environment.

It will not engage in "immoral" though perfectly legal activities.

It will not make "unfair' deals. It will not take the rural poor for a "ride'.

Though working within the existing economic framework it recognises and indeed gives priority to social objectives.

It does not regard spiritual activities as "uneconomic".

It ensures that village savings circulate within the village. It does not "drain the village resources" for the urban life.

It sees to it that the village manages its own savings and is not subservient to any other outside "source of power". There are many village banks managed entirely by the village.

These are only a few of such characteristics which come to my mind.

Lecture Nine:
Peace through Sarvodaya Social Order

Notes:

AN ANALYSIS OF THE PRESENT SOCIAL ORDER
IN RELATION TO
THE DESIRED SARVODAYA SOCIAL ORDER

Present Order

1. LACKS SELF-KNKOWLEDGE AND SELF RELIANCE
2. BLINDLY FOLLOWS MATERIALISTIC VALUES
3. WORKSHIP WEALTH POWER AND POSITION AND USES UNTRUTH, VIOLENCE AND SELFISHNESS
4. ORGANISATIONS BASED ON POSSESSION AND VICIOUS COMPETITION BECOME STRONG CAPITALISTIC ECONOMY, BUREAUCRATIC CONTROL POWER AND PARTY POLITICS BECOME MAJOR SOCIAL FORCES
5. EVIL IN MAN IS HARNESSED SOCIETY GETS FRAGMENTED INTO CASTE, RACIAL, RELIGIOUS AND PARTY-POLITICAL DIFFERENCES
6. ECONOMIC RESOURCES ARE IMPROPERLY UTILISED ECONOMY BECOMES WEAK UNEMPLOYMENT INCREASES
7. DEPENDENCE ON AN IMPORT-EXPORT ECONOMY BASED ON COLONIALLY INHERITED PATTERNS OF PRODUCTION OF CASH CROPS FOREIGN DEBTS INCREASE
8. SUBJUGATED TO LARGE SCALE ORGANISATIONS HUMAN LABOUR WASTED CORRUPTION INCREASES ENVIRONMENT IS POLLUTED
9. VILLAGES ARE SUBSERVIENT TO THE CITIES, RURAL EXODUS, MORAL DEGENERATION, SOCIAL UNREST
10. POWER OF THE STATE AND OF THE LAWS OF PUNISHMENT INCREASE LAWS OF RIGHTEOUSNESS AND PEOPLE'S POWER WEAKENS.

Desired Order

1. STRIVES FOR SELF-REALISATION AND SELF RELIANCE
2. MOTIVATED BY INDIGENOUS CULTURAL AND VALUES
3. RESPECTS VIRTUE, WISDOM AND SKILLS AND USES TRUTH NON-VIOLENCE AND SELF DENIAL
4. ORGANISATIONS BASED SHARING AND CORPORATION BECOME POWERFUL, PEOPLE'S POLITICS BASED ON ECONOMIC TRUSTEESHIP PEOPLE'S PARTICIPATION AND PARTY-LESS AND PARTICIPATORY DEMOCRACY BECOME MAJOR SOCIAL FORCES
5. GOOD IN MAN IS HARNESSSED, SOCIETY TENDS TO GET INTEGRATED AS ONE HUMAN FAMILY ALL FORCES THAT DIVIDE PEOPLE GIVE WAY TO FORCES THAT UNITE
6. ECONOMIC RESOURCCES ARE PROPERLY COMBINED PRODUCTION INCREASES EMPLOYMENT INCREASES FULL-ENGAGEMENT SOCIETIES COME INTO BEING
7. A SELF SUFFICIENT ECONOMY BASED ON PEOPLE'S BASIC NEEDS AN ECONOMY FREE FROM FOREIGN DEBITS NATIONAL SELF RESPECT AND ECONOMIC FREEDOM
8. SMALL SCALE ORGANISATIONS LABOUR INTENSIVELY USED LESS CORRUPTION REDUCTION OF PSYCHOLOGICAL AND ENVIRONMENTAL POLLUTION
9. BALANCED VILLAGE AND URBAN AWAKENING MORAL RECONSTRUCTION
10. LAWS OF RIGHTEOUSNESS AND THE POWER OF THE PEOPLE BECOME STRONG; NO RULING CLASS PEOPLE'S POWER BECOMES SUPREME SARVODAYA IS RELEASED

PATH TO NATIONAL AWAKENING - Deshodaya

1. Establishment of spiritual, moral and cultural values at individual, family, group, village and urban community and national levels.

2. Satisfaction of Ten Basic Human Needs of people beginning with the most deprived in society laying the foundation for a Right Livelihood society

3. Bringing about social development in village and urban communities by intensifying functional development educational programme for:

    (1)   Awareness creaton and leadership buildinig

    (2)   Community participation in decision - making

    (3)   Community organisation for self - reliance and self-government

    (4)   Community education for a global non-violent social order

    (5)   Protection of cultural identity and promoting unity with diversity

    (6)   Health development

    (7)   Conflict resolution, National integration and peace

    (8)   Full realisation of fundamental human rights for women and children, rule of law

4. Re-organisation of the political poweer structure in the country on the principles of:

    (1)   Participatory democratic instutitions and

    (2)   Complete decentralisation of power to village and and community level democratic institutions.

5. Re-structuring the national economy on the principles of:

    (1)   National self-sufficiency with regard to basic human needs.

    (2)   Adoption of small scale decentralised, labour intensive appropriate tech nologies for production purposes/without destruction of nature or culture

    (3)   Replacement of existing production relationships with non-exploitative trusteeship enforced by law with a Right Livelihood Society in view

    (4)   Complete non-dependence on exploitative international economic relan tionships while promoting healthy interdependenc international economic relationships to create a just global society

    (5)   Protection of the environment and bio - diversity

Lecture Ten:
Awakening in the new millenium

Notes:

PATH TO WORLD AWAKENING - Vishvodaya

1. In all countries of the world, concerned individuals and groups initiate, promote and intensify Paurushodaya, Kutumbodaya, Grāmodaya, Nagarōdaya, Deshōdaya and Vishvōdaya movements according to their historical and cultural realities.

2. These individuals and groups should build up a close communication relationship based on both affinity and vicinity and mutually support one another to build a no - poverty and peaceful society.

3. They should build up alternative but universal value - based

   (1) Living patterns/Right Livelihood/Full-Engagement communities

   (2) Production, Distribution and consumption techniques and structures, and

   (3) Assist one another to break through existing ideological barriers and political boundaries to create interdependent just societies.

   (4) They should show by example, how to build up non-violent defence mechanisms and oppose all forms of piling up of mass destruction armaments in their countries.

   (5) They should oppose all form of production that result in destruction of nature and bio-diversity, enslavement of women and children, increase poverty and bring about economic imbalances, pollution of the environment and psychological and economic impoverishment of communities anywhere in the world.

VISHVODAYA PROGRAMMES

"The Awakening of All", is the sublime thought of the Sarvodaya Shramadana Movement, which includes the awakening of the global communities as well. With this in view the Sarvodaya Shramadana Movement has set up the Sarvodaya Shramadana International Unit in order to achieve this long term objective.

The Programmes:

1. To arrange programmes and expose to SARVODAYA the prospective foreign visitors who belong to the following categories:
   - University students and other young interested people who want to study the Sarvodaya Shramadana Movement's development strategies, ideologies, programmes and projects as well as an alternative way of life as a part of their studies.
   - Scholars who are already in the field of development looking for alternative strategies to be researched.
   - Technical people in the field of development attached to various international organisations, NGOs in the Asia Pacific Region who are interested in a cross pollination experience.
   - Individuals who are interested in a different approach to development

2. Co-ordinating programmes of various volunteers who join the Sarvodaya Shramadana Movement belonging to the following categories.
   - Sponsored and non-sponsored volunteers from overseas

3. Co-ordinating the Link-Up Programme. Under this Programme a link between the communities in the villages in Sri Lanka and organisations and individuals in other countries is established with a view to promote a meaningful dialogue, so that they could help and learn from each other..

4. Promoting Sarvodaya Groups overseas and co-ordinating activities.

5. Despatch of Sarvodaya volunteers to work in other countries.

6. Promote Cultural Tourism to visiting groups and individuals.

7. Organising study tours for Sarvodaya volunteers to other countries.

8. Organising international work-shops, seminars, conferences etc., and talks and dialogues by visiting scholars and participants.

9. Promote information exchange and other similar exchanges.

Note:

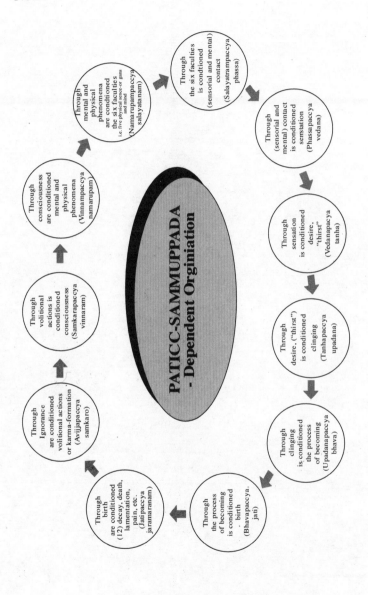

PATICC-SAMMUPPADA - Dependent Orgimiation

Through Ignorance are conditioned volitional actions or karma-formation (Avijjapaccya samkaro)

Through volitional actions is conditioned consciousness (Samkarapacya vinnaram)

Through consciousness are conditioned mental and physical phenomena (Vinnampaccya namarupam)

Through mental and physical phenomena are conditioned the six faculties i.e. five physical sense-or gans and mind (Namarupampaccya salayatanam)

Through the six faculties is conditioned (sensorial and mental) contact (Salayatrampaccya phassa)

Through (sensorial and mental) contact is conditioned sensation (Phassapaccya vedana)

Through sensation is conditioned desire, "thirst" (Vedanapaccya tanha)

Through desire, ("thirst") is conditioned clinging (Tanhapaccya upadana)

Through clinging is conditioned the process of becoming (Upadanapaccya bhava)

Through the process of becoming is conditioned birth (Bhavapaccya, jati)

Through birth are conditioned (12) decay, death, lamentation, pain, etc. (Jatipaccya jaramaranam)